1. A Time for Faith

A TIME
for
FAITH

In the Words of St. Paul and James Alberione, SSP, STD

Translation by the Daughters of St. Paul

ST. PAUL EDITIONS

NIHIL OBSTAT:
   Rev. Richard V. Lawlor, S.J.
   Censor Deputatus

IMPRIMATUR:
   + Humberto Cardinal Medeiros
   Archbishop of Boston

Library of Congress Cataloging in Publication Data

Main entry under title:

A Time for Faith.

   1. Faith — Quotations, maxims, etc.   I.   Alberione,
Giacomo Giuseppe, 1884-1971.   II.   Bible.   N.T.
Epistles of Paul.   English.   New American.   Selections.
1978.
BT772.T56   231'.2   78-6068

Photo credits:

M. Kling — 142-143
Vincent Mancusi — 8-9, 12, 14-15, 18, 20, 23, 26-27, 32, 38, 44,
      46-47, 50, 55, 56-57, 62, 64, 70-71, 90-91, 96-97, 104, 106,
      110, 117, 119, 120-121, 126, 130, 132, 134-135, 136, 140,
      146, 149, 152, 154-155, Cover
Media Center — 78-79
Sahata — 85

Printed in U.S.A. by the Daughters of St. Paul
50 St. Paul's Ave., Boston, Ma. 02130

The Daughters of St. Paul are an international
religious congregation serving the Church with the
communications media.

CONTENTS

INTRODUCTION

"A spiritual life requires a continual exercise of faith, hope and charity. Only by the light of faith and by meditation on the word of God can one always and everywhere recognize God in whom 'we live, and move, and have our being' (Acts 17:28), seek His will in every event, see Christ in everyone whether he be a relative or a stranger, and make correct judgments about the true meaning and value of temporal things both in themselves and in their relation to man's final goal.

"They who have this faith live in the hope of the revelation of the sons of God and keep in mind the cross and resurrection of the Lord. In the pilgrimage of this life, hidden with Christ in God and free from enslavement to wealth, they aspire to those riches which remain forever and generously dedicate themselves wholly to the advancement of the kingdom of God and to the reform and improvement of the temporal order in a Christian spirit. Among the trials of this life they find strength in hope, convinced that 'the sufferings of the present time are not worthy to be compared with the glory to come that will be revealed in us' (Rom. 8:18)" (Apostolicam Actuositatem, 4).

We must "follow the poor Christ, the humble and cross-bearing Christ in order to be worthy of being sharers in His glory. Every person must walk unhesitatingly according to his own personal gifts and duties in the path of living faith, which arouses hope and works through charity" (Lumen Gentium, 40).

"The witness of a living and mature faith [is] one trained to see difficulties and to master them.... This faith needs to prove its fruitfulness by penetrating the believer's entire life, including its worldly dimensions, and by activating him toward justice and love..." (Gaudium et Spes, 21).

This collection of thoughts will be a great aid in the renewal of our lives—in living our pilgrimage here in faith and courage, walking in the footsteps of our Savior, Jesus Christ, of His Mother and the saints to eternal life, where "we shall see face to face..." (1 Cor. 13:12) the God we now see through the eyes of faith.

A Hymn

to Faith

Faith is the light
that illumines our journey toward heaven.
It is faith that makes the Christian
different from the philosopher,
just as reason distinguishes man from animals.
The knowledge which comes from revelation is
     more perfect,
more sublime and more secure than the
     knowledge
which comes from the intellect or the senses.

Faith leads us to share in the wisdom of God
and unites us to Him.
The light with which God knows Himself
then becomes our light;
the wisdom of God, our wisdom;
His mind, our mind;
His will, our will;
His life, our life.

Faith is the source of true light for our minds,
strength and consolation for our wills
and of merit for our souls.

By faith the intellect rests on God, on the
    divine.
How much God has revealed about His mysteries,
about the indwelling of the Holy Spirit,
about the purpose of our lives,
about the reward for the good
and the punishment for the bad;
and even more about the principles
and means which help us
to reach eternal life.

Faith is our only source
of strength and consolation.
It helps us think of our eternal reward:
"From now on a merited crown awaits me"
    (2 Tm. 4:8), says St. Paul.
And elsewhere, "I consider the sufferings
    of the present
to be as nothing compared with the glory
to be revealed in us" (Rom. 8:18).

And so a person struggles;
he or she battles passions;
he or she fulfills his or her daily duty
    with courage:
"...the power that has conquered the world
is this faith of ours" (1 Jn. 5:4).

12

Lack of supernatural knowledge, or
intellectual pride, or a life of vice are the reasons
why many do not believe, or have a weak
    faith,
which is powerless in the face of temptation
or of its enemies.

Faith is a gift of God;
therefore, we must pray for an increase of it.
With prayer and exercise,
faith will become stronger, more effective, more
    illumined.

In this manner, faith can be brought to
    perfection,
that is, to the point of living it:
"My just man will live by faith" (Heb. 10:38).

Faith,

a Gift of God

"It is owing to his favor
that salvation is yours through faith.
This is not your own doing, it is God's gift;
neither is it a reward for anything you have
    accomplished,
so let no one pride himself on it.
We are truly his handiwork, created in Christ
    Jesus
to lead the life of good deeds
which God prepared for us in advance."

—Ephesians 2:8-10

"In him [Jesus] you too were chosen;
when you heard the glad tidings of salvation,
the word of truth,
and believed in it,

you were sealed with the Holy Spirit
who had been promised.
He is the pledge of our inheritance,
the first payment against the full redemption
of a people God has made his own,
to praise his glory."

—Ephesians 1:13-14

"This treasure we possess in earthen vessels
to make it clear that its surpassing power
comes from God and not from us."

—2 Corinthians 4:7

"Faith is...conviction about things we do not see."

—Hebrews 11:1

2. A Time for Faith

Faith is a theological virtue
infused by God in our hearts
which inclines us to believe firmly in the truths
revealed by Him and proposed for our
        acceptance by His Church.
One believes with the help of divine grace,
not because he already understands these truths,
but because they are revealed by God,
who cannot err or deceive us.

Faith is free adhesion to revealed truth;
therefore, it requires effort on our part.

We are headed toward eternal life.
After faith, we shall have vision.
In heaven faith disappears because we see God.
If we wish to attain to the vision of God
we must prepare ourselves.
Our present life is a preparation for heaven.

The light of reason reaches
only as far as philanthrophy;
the light of faith widens its horizons
as far as eternity.

God raised man to the supernatural order,
bestowing upon him divine grace;
a free gift because it is grace.
And this grace, reflecting itself on the
    intelligence,
produces faith.

To believe: this is a gift of the Holy Spirit.
It was about upright souls
that the Divine Master declared:
"Father, Lord of heaven and earth,
to you I offer praise;
for what you have hidden from the learned and
    the clever
you have revealed to the merest children"
    (Mt. 11:25).

Many of those who lived at the time of Jesus
did not want to recognize even His miracles.
Those who did recognize Him
became sons of God in Christ.
Even today, not all people accept the doctrine,
morals, sacraments and Gospel of Christ.
He is, as He always was, a sign of contradiction.
The humble welcome His kingship like children,
    with simplicity;
the proud, instead, do not have the gift of faith.

Faith is the greatest good:
it is the beginning of eternal salvation
and the foundation and root of justification
    and of grace.
"Without faith, it is impossible to please him
    [God]" (Heb. 11:6).
No one possesses grace without faith.

Faith is the positive foundation of every virtue,
the principle of Christian life, the gateway to
    the sacraments.
Our faith is the measure
of our possession of the other virtues.

Religion, in the first place, is faith.
We do not have hope, and much less charity,
if we do not have faith.
Charity is in proportion to faith.

To achieve perfect love of God, there must be
a proportionate depth of faith.
Without the foundation of faith,
love cannot last; it is merely sentimentalism.
Faith must be the primary basis of all religion.
Then comes hope in the merits of Jesus Christ
and imitation of Him;
and, finally, love of God, grace—
the life of God in us—
prayer and the liturgy.

Faith is not a reasoning process.
It is not even a feeling;
no, it is a gift of God,
a heavenly light which shines in the soul.

Infuse in me, O Divine Spirit,
a deep, constant, joyful faith.
May it be the sun of my life,
the lantern for the path to eternity,
a gift of Your tender love. .

I Believe,

Lord...

"Anyone who comes to God
must believe that he exists,
and that he rewards those who seek him."

—Hebrews 11:6

"For if you confess with your lips that
    Jesus is Lord,
and believe in your heart that God raised
    him from the dead,
you will be saved.
Faith in the heart leads to justification,
confession on the lips to salvation.
Scripture says, 'No one who believes in him
will be put to shame.'
Everyone who calls on the name of the Lord
will be saved."

—Romans 10:9-11, 13

"Each of you is a son of God
because of your faith in Christ Jesus."

—Galatians 3:26

"It is in the spirit that we eagerly await
the justification we hope for,
and only faith can yield it.

In Christ Jesus neither circumcision
nor the lack of it counts for anything;
only faith, which expresses itself through love."

— Galatians 5:5-6

"We preach Christ crucified — a stumbling
    block to Jews,
and an absurdity to Gentiles;
but to those who are called, Jews and Greeks
    alike,
Christ the power of God and the wisdom of God.
For God's folly is wiser than men,
and his weakness more powerful than men."

— 1 Corinthians 1:23-25

"Now that we have been justified by faith,
we are at peace with God through our Lord
    Jesus Christ.
Through him we have gained access by faith
to the grace in which we now stand,
and we boast of our hope for the glory of God."

— Romans 5:1-2

St. Paul wrote to the Galatians:
"May I never boast of anything but the cross
of our Lord Jesus Christ" (Gal. 6:14).
The cross is the symbol of the passion of
     Jesus Christ,
and therefore the symbol of that work of salvation
which came to us by means of His redemptive
     sacrifice.

By faith we see that all human and religious
    knowledge
must be reduced to the statement of St. Paul:
"To know Christ and him crucified"
    (cf. 1 Cor. 2:2).

The Son of God became man to save sinful man.
This was His constant concern:
to save, bringing truth, holiness,
and worship of the true God.

At least once in a while every Christian
must make some positive act of faith,
but especially at the point of death,
in dangers, and during temptations
against the Faith.

A person may believe that to pick up a book
    on faith
is simply a study, an instruction.
But it has a goal, a scope:
that of knowing more perfectly Jesus Christ,
the doctrine that He preached
and which is taught by His Church.
Thus one will have a purer faith,
a wider, more profound faith.
May instruction be ever more profound!

The person of character is he who possesses
    strong convictions
and endeavors firmly and consistently
to conform his life to them.

Light for the

World

"Preaching the gospel
is not the subject of a boast;
I am under compulsion and have no choice.
I am ruined if I do not preach it."

—1 Corinthians 9:16

"I am not ashamed of the gospel.
It is the power of God
leading everyone who believes in it
to salvation....,"

—Romans 1:16

"It is not ourselves we preach
but Christ Jesus as Lord,
and ourselves as your servants
for Jesus' sake.
For God, who said,

'Let light shine out of darkness,'
has shone in our hearts,
that we in turn might make known
the glory of God shining on the face of Christ."

—2 Corinthians 4:5-6

"You can depend on this
as worthy of complete acceptance.
This explains why we work and struggle as we do;
our hopes are fixed on the living God
who is the savior of all men,
but especially of those who believe.
Such are the things you must urge and teach."

—1 Timothy 4:9-11

"The Lord stood by my side
and gave me strength,
so that through me the preaching task
might be completed and all the nations
might hear the gospel."

—2 Timothy 4:17

Paul carried his faith to the farthest limits
    of the world.
He proclaimed it to shepherds, to mountaineers,
to the civilized nations of the time:
to Galatians, Corinthians, Thessalonians,
    Ephesians.
And his voice was heard in Athens and in Rome,
in Jerusalem and all over the Orient.

His doctrine was so clear,
his faith so lively,
that he both persuaded and conquered.
Because of this, St. John Chrysostom rightly
    exclaimed
that Paul carried all peoples in his heart,
and that the people were lacking to him,
but not he to the people.

Let us be people of faith in order to live it
    and share it with our neighbor;
let us remember that as brightly as our lamps
    are lit,
so much will they send forth light.
"You are the light of the world" (Mt. 5:14).
One does not light a lamp and then put it
    under a bushel,
but puts it on a lampstand
so that it gives light to all (cf. Mt. 5:15).
One does not use a piece of ice to light a fire,
but rather something which will ignite.
We will light up others
to the degree that we ourselves are "lit"
by the love of God.

We must remember that we have just one work
    to accomplish,
though this has different applications.
We must grow in faith,
to nourish our hope
and stir up our love of God and of our neighbor.
Herein lies perfection.
The person who draws close to God
thereby draws even closer to other people!
The individual who feels God and speaks to Him
with a certain intimacy
is renewed in strength
and at the same time is inflamed with zeal for
    others.

Martyrdom is rare nowadays,
but at every minute we have to conquer human
    respect.
We must profess the Gospel with courage,
in the eyes of a world
which refuses to receive it
because it knows nothing about it.

If one had only the reasoning
of those who think solely in a materialistic way
and did not elevate his or her mind
to consider everything in the spirit of the
    redemption,
then it would happen that that person
would become blind, live without faith,
and lack apostolic spirit.
Therefore, heavenly light must guide us,
and we must often recall the fundamentals
    of our Faith.

We have a soul to save.
There is a world to save,
this poor world that goes on losing its faith,
because too many are the teachers
who continually spread evil and error.
Let us use the same means they do
to teach truth, justice, and virtue.

It is faith that saves.
And in order to reach salvation,
one needs to believe in the eternal truths,
the gravity of sin,
and the divinity of the Founder of the Church.
The author of the letter to the Hebrews writes:
"In times past, God spoke in fragmentary
and varied ways
to our fathers through the prophets;
in this, the final age, he has spoken to us
through his Son" (Heb. 1:1).

In giving His divine Son to mankind,
God gave it His Word—a great gift!
The apostles carried His message,
His Gospel of peace,
through the apostolate of preaching:
"Their voice has sounded over the whole earth,
and their words to the limits of the world"
    (Rom. 10:18).

It is not difficult to tell someone
that he or she should believe,
but it is a wholly complex and difficult task
to give simultaneously an example of faith
and of every virtue
and to obtain grace for them by prayer.

We all have a mission in life,
according to our own state in life.
One day Jesus Christ will ask of us an account
    of this mission.
We will have to answer for it to God,
and the one who has not only done well,
but has also taught others to do so,
will have a greater reward in heaven.

Practice

"You must hold fast to faith,
be firmly grounded and steadfast in it,
unshaken in the hope promised you by the
    gospel...."

—Colossians 1:23

"Take care, my brothers, lest any of you
have an evil and unfaithful spirit
and fall away from the living God.
Encourage one another daily
while it is still 'today,'
so that no one grows hardened by the deceit
    of sin.
We have become partners of Christ
only if we maintain to the end
that confidence with which we began."

—Hebrews 3:12-14

"Athletes deny themselves all sorts of things.
They do this to win a crown of leaves that
      withers,
but we a crown that is imperishable.

"I do not run like a man who loses sight
of the finish line.
I do not fight as if I were shadowboxing.
What I do is discipline my own body and
      master it,
for fear that after having preached to others
I myself should be rejected."

                      —1 Corinthians 9:25-27

Onward to the goal!
In this way we will attain heavenly glory.
Blessed is he who is faithful to the end.
Jesus will come to meet him,
and smiling will say, "Do not be afraid,
good and faithful servant;
you have been faithful to your baptismal
    promises,
to your vocation, to your mission on earth.
Do not be fearful, therefore.
Enter the joy of your Lord."

Faith is needed,
a living, constant, firm faith.
That is, a faith by which we believe
that the Lord has established a mission for us,
along with the necessary helps and graces.
It is a faith that shows itself
by a practical life—
working as if all depended on us,
and trusting in God
as if all depended on Him!

It is a truth of faith that,
whether our lives are long or short,
we can save ourselves.
See how far your faith must go—
to believing that notwithstanding our sins,
we can become holy.

The person who has faith thinks often of heaven,
of the Lord and of the eternal reward.
He says often, "What I do now is a little thing,
but the prize will be in eternity!"
Little to suffer, eternal the joy;
little the work, eternal the prize!
The Lord will reward in full measure.
Our hearts are too small to enjoy eternity,
but God will enlarge them
because the happiness enjoyed by the soul
    will be very great.

Let us recall the duties of our baptism:
to believe,
to observe the divine law,
to serve God.
Thinking of this
we can make an examination of conscience
that embraces the whole complex of duties
which good Christians have.

Do not sin with thoughts.
Let there be vigilance over the mind,
in order to avoid vanity, twisted judgments,
    vain ends.
Have instead faith in God,
the thought of heaven,
of that beautiful paradise which God has
    created for us.

If one would reason things out,
he would never sin.
Every time we sin we are acting foolishly,
and we are not using our reason well.
Moreover, in that moment
we also show our lack of faith.

Onward, onward, always towards the goal.
Live in the presence of God,
hunger and thirst for His Word,
love the Gospel.
The life of faith brings us also to the desire
to grow in grace, and to use all the means
    to do so.
It brings us to the grace
of perfecting our union with God in Jesus Christ.

"Go; your faith has saved you" (cf. Lk. 17:19).
Jesus gives graces in proportion to this faith,
    this trust.
Nothing is denied to him who asks with faith,
neither spiritual nor material goods.
He who has confidence commands God.

The Spirit

of Faith

"...I still live my human life,
but it is a life of faith in the Son of God...."
—Galatians 2:20

"We have that spirit of faith
of which the Scripture says,
'Because I believed, I spoke out.'
We believe and so we speak,
knowing that he who raised up the Lord Jesus
will raise us up along with Jesus
and place both us and you in his presence.
Indeed, everything is ordered to your benefit,
so that the grace bestowed in abundance
may bring greater glory to God
because they who give thanks are many."
—   —2 Corinthians 4:13-15

"We do not lose heart,
because our inner being is renewed each day
even though our body is being destroyed at the
    same time.
The present burden of our trial is light enough,
and earns for us an eternal weight of glory
    beyond all comparison.
We do not fix our gaze on what is seen
but on what is unseen.
What is seen is transitory;
what is unseen lasts forever."

—2 Corinthians 4:16-18

How can the spirit of faith be defined?
The spirit of faith is
a profound persuasion about revealed truth,
and the practical and constant exercise of faith.
It must be impressed on all our sentiments and
    words.
The house of God is founded on faith,
is raised up on hope,
and is completed by love.
Therefore, our own spiritual edifice is founded
    on faith,
elevated on Christian hope in the future reward,
and accomplished with charity and works inspired
    by it.

When the foundation is strong,
it should be able to support a good edifice, a
     magnificent structure.
If instead the foundation is weak,
the edifice cannot be great.
Consider how you stand in regard to your
     spiritual foundation.

Coming more to the concrete,
the spirit of faith animates the soul and the
     body.
Why does the dishonest person act the way
     he does?
Why does the drunkard act as he does?
And what prompts pride?
It comes from the spirit of pride, from gluttony
     or from avarice.
Why does pride exalt itself?
Why speak that way, work in that manner, go
     there or come here?
Because pride is moved by the *spirit of pride.*

Now we will turn to reflection on the example
    of a saint.
Francis de Sales was held in contempt for
    four years,
forced to be a fugitive, and to live as a
    wanderer,
subjected to every kind of suffering and
    persecution,
and even hunted down by those seeking his
    life.
Yet he did not stop—ever—
and in the end he was fully rewarded.

The soul and the body are guided
by the spirit according to which one lives.
If the spirit is good, it will bring us to good;
if the spirit is bad, it will lead us to evil.

What does the mind do?
What does our brain project?
What are the desires of our heart?
How are our words?
They are according to the spirit within us.

We make acts of faith;
I mean to say, once in a while,
given the opportunity,
we express our consent to the truths revealed
    by God
and those which the Church proposes to us.
But the spirit of faith is something more
    profound.
It extends to all the convictions held by the mind,
so that it inspires and guides ideas, reasonings,
    judgments, desires,
and the aspirations and affections of the heart....
It is found in the Christian, who, with the spirit
    of faith,
reasons according to revealed principles.
Everything is seen under this aspect.

Faith enters into all the convictions of the mind,
and then descends into the heart, soul and all
    the sentiments;
it inspires holy works,
the works of zeal, the heroism of Christian life.

Faith is the root
from which the trunk grows,
expands into branches,
bears leaves,
flowers and fruit.

What kind of a spirit can a Christian have,
who in his conversations shows that he reasons
like a materialist?
What kind of studies are those accomplished
for purely material ends?
What kind of works are those done according
to earthly interests,
in the desire for monetary profit,
in the spirit of vanity or of sensuality?
Even religious acts done by someone with this
spirit are like corpses—without a soul.

How much we must humiliate ourselves
if we reason too humanly,
if our conversations are inspired by worldly
    principles,
if our sentiments are worldly,
if our works are like those of persons who do
    not value what is eternal.

The *spirit of faith* is more than faith.
It is not enough to admire the beauty of faith;
Rousseau writes: "I confess that in reading
    the Bible
I felt caught up by its beauty;
the holiness of the Gospel moved me."
And yet, what was his life like?
A heap of errors and scandals.
Admiration must also be manifested
in works conformable to a perfect Christian
    life.

Several young men in Paris heard these words
    many years ago:
"What profit would a man show if he were to
    gain the whole world
and destroy himself in the process?
What can a man offer in exchange for his very
    self?" (Mt. 16:26)
And yet only St. Francis Xavier went on to
    accomplish great works.

St. Ignatius, his superior, asked him if he would
    be disposed to leave for India,
to evangelize the natives.
St. Francis, although he had many good projects
    planned
and many works of zeal already started,
looked at his Father with reverence, and
    responded:
"I will go, taking only my breviary."
He did not ask how he would go or who he
    would have for a companion
or how he must go about it.
With such ardor, in those savage places, he
    began his mission!
The love that he had for Jesus Christ,
the heart he had for souls,
enflamed him with the desire to save souls, even
    in that uncivilized place.
This was the spirit of faith!

Faith must be lived especially in its most
    essential point,
that is, the spiritual value of our lives.
We must understand our essence.
In other words, why did God create me?

We came forth from the creative hand of God.
For a short time we remain here, as exiles
    from heaven,
and then we return to God, to the Father.
We must, therefore, look toward heaven.

If this supernatural truth—
which is the greatest principle for the direction
      of life—
is not what regulates our life,
we do not have the spirit of faith.
We may at times make some acts of faith,
but our faith will not become action:
"Faith without works is as dead as a body
      without breath" (Jas. 2:26).

This is the work of every person that lives:
to direct all toward eternity,
choosing what will most readily insure salvation.
This is the first moral principle,
an obvious principle, one which must guide us.
This is the principle which must be uppermost
among our practical reasonings: life is for
      heaven;
if, therefore, an action will help me to reach
      paradise, I must perform it.
If it will not bring me to heaven, I must not
      do it.

Let us ask our Lady for the spirit of faith.
Let us pray that the Holy Spirit will descend
    on us,
shedding His heavenly grace.
Then our thoughts, sentiments and works
will be inspired by the principles of faith.
He who has the spirit of faith is powerful—
in his works, in his words, in his virtue,
in his nearness to God, in his relations with men.
Although very weak, he can be greater than a
    learned person,
more powerful than a captain,
more able than a politician, if these lack in faith.
Faith grows strong in hope,
expands in charity and bears fruit in eternal life.

Faith and

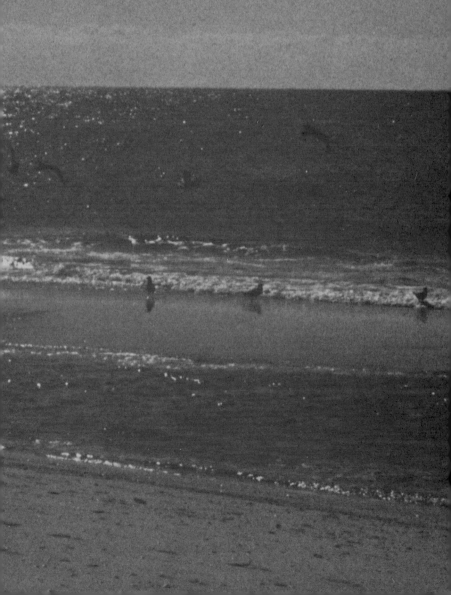

the Person

"Therefore I am content with weakness,
with mistreatment, with distress,
with persecutions and difficulties
for the sake of Christ;
for when I am powerless, it is then that I
　　am strong."

— 2 Corinthians 12:10

"In him who is the source of my strength
I have strength for everything."

— Philippians 4:13

"May the God of our Lord Jesus Christ, the
     Father of glory,
grant you a spirit of wisdom and insight to
     know him clearly.
May he enlighten your innermost vision
that you may know the great hope to which he
     has called you...
and the immeasurable scope of his power in us
     who believe."

                             —Ephesians 1:17-18, 19

The Spirit makes thoughts sublime and holy.
He also sanctifies wills and hearts.

Faith makes our minds holy.
The mind is very powerful.
Although our brain is such a small member
    of the body
(it would fit easily in a compact box),
the world, vast as it is,
would take up only a tiny corner of the human
    brain.
The mind imagines other worlds,
transcends all of nature
and reaches to the outermost limits of space.

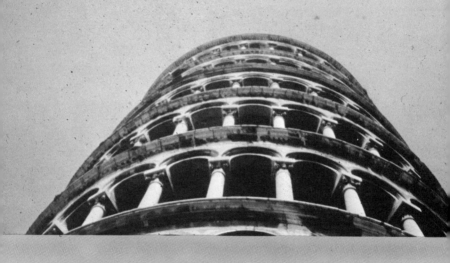

The spirit of faith must illumine our mind.
If by nature the reason is very powerful,
through the spirit of faith,
the Christian can elevate himself above reason;
he can see above time to eternity,
and above earthly things to the supernatural.
Faith makes us believe in God's Providence in
    all things.

There should be a constant optimism
founded on divine Providence
which, by calling us to sanctity,
always disposes the necessary means, occasions,
    trials and consolations,
with wisdom and love.
"I cannot learn"; "I will never understand";
"There are too many difficulties"....
These expressions will never be heard from
    a person
who has the spirit of faith.

The hour of God sounds;
for me it is enough to do my part,
and to God goes the success and the glory—
in the manner and at the time He wills.

The spirit of faith elevates a person to the
    most sublime heights;
it makes us trust and believe in the grace of
    the Holy Spirit.
The spirit of faith inspires us to remain in
    church with respect,
and has us utilize time
as a treasure for eternity.

The Lord calls us sometimes
to very high missions and very beautiful things,
but this exacts much faith.
If we acquire this spirit of faith,
we will correspond to His call....

To one without faith,
the present time is to be enjoyed
and the goods of the earth are the treasures
  he searches for.
Oh, let us have faith!
Let us not lose ourselves, as some do,
with human arguments or with the preoccupa-
  tions of the "ego."
These things will leave us with empty hearts
and, especially at the point of death, with a great
  sorrow.

Faith sanctifies our wills.
The spirit of faith animates the will,
that is, it makes a person count on divine help,
and choose the works of God,
looking toward Him in all things.
Looking only at our possibilities,
natural talents and human resources,
we many times lose courage,
since we think it is presumption to perform
  certain works
depending solely on our own strength.

But the spirit of faith
brings us to count on God, to pray;
he who hopes in God will not be confounded:
"And this hope will not leave us disappointed"

—Romans 5:5

6. A Time for Faith

What is impossible to men is possible to God.
Do, therefore, what is "impossible" for you,
and by God's grace, it will become possible
due to His mercy and power.
Cannot God, who has created everything,
do also that which is definitely smaller?

Cannot God, who is the transformer and
    sanctifier of apostles,
transform us and make His grace powerful in
    us, too?

When one counts on God—
although he will suffer at certain times
and feel discouraged—
God will not abandon him in the battle.
God will be with him!
Yes, the Church is continually cast into the
    tempest,
but Jesus Christ is in the bark;
whenever He wants,
He commands the winds and the waves,
and calm and tranquillity return to the sea.

We must count on the Lord,
for He gives grace to whoever depends on Him.
In the spiritual life,
we must fight our passions:
anger, envy, pride, the flesh;
they must be subdued in order to make them
    submissive to reason
and to the spirit.
Who can hope to conquer them?
He who counts on the grace of God.
In the work of perfection we must grow in
    virtue daily.
Who can be confident of constant progress?
He who counts on God.
In the apostolate
we find before us obstacles of every kind.
Who will be the Lord's faithful servant?
He who counts on God,
because graces are prepared for everyone
according to his state in life.

In life, he who has faith
chooses works which are spiritually nobler and
thus more meritorious.
He does not care for temporal gains;
he does not look for esteem;
he is not guided by the passions.

His greatest principles are:
to work for the greater glory of God;
to seek, above all, the reign of God and the
    salvation of souls,
elevating them to greater spiritual perfection;
to prefer what is poorest;
to desire to be despised and forgotten;
to keep present the Last Things and provide
    for eternity.

Faith makes the soul ready for the acquisition of
    every virtue.
Just as when the foundation is missing,
an edifice cannot be sustained,
so he who does not have faith cannot have
    other virtues.
He who has little faith
will arrive at the point of exercising some
    virtue,
perhaps performing some virtuous acts.
But he who has great faith
will exercise virtue with justice;
that is, each one in its own time,
each one in its own place
and each virtue practiced in its own specific
    area.

Those who are just in relation to God
fulfill the debt of honor, glory, and worship
    due Him.
Faith makes us honor God
as Creator and Author of every good;
faith shows God as Ruler,
provident and wise;
faith makes us consider Him
as the all-good One, our eternal happiness.

Faith sanctifies our hearts.
The first sentiment we need is a lively desire
    for heaven:
"I long to be freed from this life
and to be with Christ," says St. Paul (Phil. 1:23).
His ardent love for Christ
made him yearn for the moment of death,
when the bonds of the body would be broken
and the soul could fly freely
into the embrace of Jesus Christ.

By faith we see this life as an exile,
and heaven as our beloved homeland;
we see the many dangers of the present life

and the glorious security of the blessed in
     heaven;
the vanity of the goods of the earth,
and the complete happiness that is found in God.

Faith excites sorrow for sin;
it unveils the greatness of God
and the deformity of rebellion against His infinite
    majesty.
Faith makes us understand
the many benefits of the Lord
and the black ingratitude of the one who
    offends Him.
Faith shows us the crucified Jesus
as the victim of sin,
and brings tears of love, compassion and
    repentance.
Faith makes us understand
the value of grace and of friendship with God.
It points out the ruin, the destruction,
which sin causes in the soul.
Faith moves one to greater fervor and love
    for God.
The missal, the sacramentary and the breviary
    or Christian Prayer
are the guiding principles for prayer,
especially liturgical prayer.
But where do the sentiments expressed
in the psalms, the prayers of the Church, and
    liturgical hymns, come from?

From a lively, heartfelt faith,
nourished by meditation.
What sentiments of faith and love
there are in that short prayer, "Soul of Christ"!

Faith also excites ardor for the sanctification
    of one's soul.
And it is faith that makes known to us
the value of the gifts of the Holy Spirit,
the beatitudes, the fruits of grace.

The spirit of faith dominates the mind, the
    will, the heart.
It is the foundation of the supernatural man,
of the Christian, the religious, the priest.
The spirit of faith is a gift of God.
The most beautiful fruit it produces
is the apostle on earth,
and the saint in heaven.

Growth

"We pray for you always
that our God may make you worthy of his call,
and fulfill by his power
every honest intention and work of faith.
In this way the name of our Lord Jesus
may be glorified...."

— 2 Thessalonians 1:11-12

"May the God of peace
make you perfect in holiness.
May he preserve you whole and entire,
spirit, soul, and body,
irreproachable at the coming of our Lord Jesus
   Christ.
He who calls us is trustworthy,
therefore he will do it."

— 1 Thessalonians 5:23-24

In every state in life,
in every time,
in every circumstance,
we must ask the Lord
for the grace of thoughts, works and sentiments
according to faith.
Let us relish, think of and look for whatever
is supernatural.
Earth is a preparation for heaven,
where faith will end,
and the fruits of our life will ripen.

We must prepare our minds
for the vision of God with faith;
we must prepare our hearts
to savor the divine;
and we must prepare our wills
for the possession of God.
Herein, therefore, is found the most beautiful
fruit of faith:
eternal salvation and one's sanctification.

The negative means for growth in faith
are those which preserve us
from what endangers faith.
Our faith runs many risks.

When we are fervent,
we do not notice the dangers.
While we read lives of the saints,
while we consider spiritual things,
we feel inflamed,
full of fervor,
full of good will.
We then begin to count on ourselves,
challenging dangers and difficulties.
And then?

We ourselves notice
that the lamp is smoldering,
its splendor fades
and it seems that it will be extinguished.
What is this?

It is the rising wind;
it is the mixing of water with oil;
it is the tempest that rages all around us.

Then we do not see any more;
our North Star is no longer in view;
we lose sight of the direction of our life;
we no longer recall the true end of our
    existence.
Our souls are continually nourished by God
with delicate food:
the Word of God,
the Eucharistic bread
and the study of sacred subjects.
Why then are not all our thoughts holy and
    supernatural?
Often the reason is
human respect and human weakness,
whereby one lacks the courage
to manifest the spirit that is in us.
Even between persons who think they are
    spiritual,
some amount of human respect reigns.
Also idleness of the mind and heart
constitute a danger for the faith,
because: "Idleness is a teacher of many evils."
Be occupied! What a great help for the spirit,
for conserving fervor,
for keeping the fire of our spiritual life warm,
for keeping the lamp of our faith
continually lit and well fueled.

He who has the light of faith
sees God in all things —
simply and discerningly (cf. Mt. 6:22-23).
The eye of faith makes the way clear.
Walk in the light so that the darkness
will not make the way obscure
and so that you will not fall into dangers.

Become simple in your thoughts.
Let your entire thought be dominated by God,
and see all things in relation to Him.
St. Francis de Sales used to say:
"I have only a few desires and,
if I could be born again,
I would have only one: God."
This is simplicity.
The person who truly seeks God in everything
achieves the life of union with Him.

Readings on the lives of the saints,
readings from spiritual books,
reading and studying well done
on sacred subjects
and on secular topics—
oh! how much these contribute to spiritual
   progress!
They are like continual prayer
which obtains the grace of faith.
It is not study or knowledge
which constitutes faith,
but prayer that obtains the increase of faith.
If one reads and studies with the same spirit
as one receives Communion,
then he will feel even more spiritual benefits.

Let us uplift and nourish ourselves
on the heavenly bread of truth.
Let us tolerate those
who must be occupied with this earth;
some are so occupied with it
that they attach their hearts to earthly things
and no longer desire heaven.
Oh! that the light of faith
may always shine brightly before us!

Even though one out of ten believes
that faith is a sentiment, it is not;
it is a gift of God, a celestial light
which illuminates the soul.

All good things are acquired with fatigue.
And should it not be that faith,
the most precious of gifts,
also require fatigue?

110

Faith is a virtue;
virtue demands strength of a person.
Faith is the first virtue;
it therefore requires a greater strength.
Faith is:
"Do what is in your power and God will aid
　　your good will."
For example, faith is a principle in life;
It is to believe that this present life
is a preparation for eternity.
We believe that everything we do
will merit a great reward;
we work as though we had already seen
that the work of "a full day in the scorching
　　heat" (Mt. 20:12)
will have its recompense.
Do we not believe
that our minimal fatigue
will merit for us great glory?

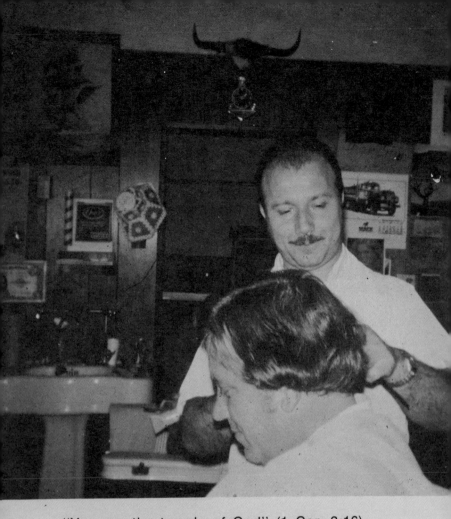

"You are the temple of God" (1 Cor. 3:16).
When we write letters, when we speak, when
    we work,
may the spirit of faith guide us.
It is a divine promise:
"The measure with which you measure
will be used to measure you" (Mt. 7:2).
Even when we must deal with material things,
let us treat of them in a supernatural spirit.
It is necessary also to pray
to acquire the spirit of faith.

Our Lord will give the good spirit
to whoever asks for it:
"What father among you will give his son
    a snake if he asks for a fish,
or hand him a scorpion if he asks for an egg?
If you, with all your sins,
know how to give your children good things,
how much more will the heavenly Father give the
    Holy Spirit
to those who ask him" (Lk. 11:11-13).

Let us pray that the Lord will sanctify our minds.
We live in a time
in which we need to love the Lord with all
    our mind.

To be persons of faith, it is necessary to believe
that there is a God, that He has created us
and that He awaits us to give us the reward
or the punishment we deserve.
We must live of faith
under the gaze of the Lord.

Acquire a greater faith.
You can see that living by faith
is not living according to reason or the senses.
It means to live guided by supernatural principles.

The communication of Jesus to every soul
takes place particularly by means of knowledge
and of faith in the Son of God made man,
in His Gospel.

The Holy Spirit is He
who reveals the divine Son to us
and increases in us His divine life
by the gifts of wisdom, understanding and love.

Have faith! My heavenly Father guards me,
    assists me:
I am His!
I work in His presence,
so that He can say of me, "He pleases me!"
Have faith in the graces
that come from the Eucharist—the Eucharistic
    Celebration,
Holy Communion and Eucharistic Visits.

Have faith that whatever happens,
whether pleasing or displeasing, comes from God.
He disposes moment by moment
that which is better for us.

Let us always remember
that it is the Lord who cares for us
and who has shown us the way
by which we can arrive at paradise.

The heavenly Father who clothes the sparrow
    with feathers
and provides it with a nest,
dresses the lilies of the field,
even numbers the hairs of our head, and
always helps those who have faith and
    pray to Him—
perhaps at the last moment, yet, on time.

God gives always what is needed—
therefore, there must be faith to obtain
and readiness to receive.

Do I have faith when faced with material
    difficulties?
Do I understand and believe strongly
in the supernatural power of the Church?
In the temptations
and in the disillusionments of life,
do I confide in Jesus Crucified, and do I pray?

For the Faith
Paul put up with scourgings, persecutions
and the pains of imprisonment.
And for this Faith he gave his own life.

Love the Gospel, Sacred Scripture,
the letters of St. Paul,
and nourish yourself daily with these sources
  of faith.
Be happy, always more united to the Lord.

Secure

in Him

"This great confidence in God is ours,
through Christ.
It is not that we are entitled of ourselves
to take credit for anything.

Our sole credit is from God,
who has made us qualified ministers of a new
        covenant,
a covenant not of a written law
but of spirit.
The written law kills,
but the Spirit gives life."

— 2 Corinthians 3:4-6

What does it mean to abandon oneself in God?
To abandon oneself in God means
to place all in His hands
in order to make our thoughts,
desires and wants one with what God wills.
It is to let oneself be guided as a child,
because if we do not become as little children,
there will not be a place for us in the kingdom
    of heaven.

Abandonment in God means to have no more
    preferences,
no more desires,
to refuse nothing and to ask nothing;
it means to let ourselves be "worked on"
    by Jesus.
Abandonment in God is not laziness;
it means accepting all that is disposed by Him.
Full abandonment in God, then,
means to embrace His will with all our heart
and to fulfill it,
applying our mind, will and heart,
and both supernatural and natural powers.
"If it pleases Jesus, it pleases me,
so I will do it as well as I can."

Is abandonment in God useful?
Truly, perfection is found in it.
This is so when one's opinion does not count
    any more,
nor one's way of seeing things, nor his desires,
nor whether he is sick or healthy.

Abandon yourselves in God as Mary did.
This is the highest peak of perfection,
since in this abandonment in God our ego is
    put to death
and Jesus lives fully in the soul:
"...the life I live now is not my own;
Christ is living in me" (Gal. 2:20).
Thus Jesus will take complete possession
    of our person
and it will be He who works totally in us.

He will work in our mind
and produce faith and knowledge of God.
He will act on our will, strengthening it
and making it lean always more toward
    what pleases Him.
He will place in our heart His own heart,
that heart which loved the Father so much
and loved me to such an extent;
that heart so humble and good,
so sensitive to the miseries of humanity,
to the troubles of souls,
and to the spiritual condition of so many
    who are unhappy.

Jesus is within us and He lets us work,
but our thoughts are His;
our mind thinks, but it is Jesus who thinks;
our arms and legs and all our being functions,
but it is Jesus who commands us and makes us
   move.

It is Jesus who makes us love the Eucharist,
makes us long for heaven,
makes us order all our thoughts and activities
toward paradise.
Then our soul experiences profound happiness
in church,
at the celebration of or participation
in the Liturgy.

Two persons are living here—
the person still lives,
but in him lives Jesus.
Two persons, but only one spirit,
for the soul is transformed into Christ.
"God became man so that man could become
God."
And now, neither life nor death,
nor the sword, nor prison, nor sickness,
hunger, nor thirst
can separate us from God,
because we are abandoned in Him.
St. Paul challenged all creation to separate
him from God,
so much did he feel himself welded onto Christ.
This abandonment in God is, therefore,
perfection.

The enemy of this abandonment in God is
    always our ego,
which manifests itself in our thoughts,
sentiments or the activity of our wills.
Many times between us and Jesus there is a
    certain battle —
between this ego that goes on living
and Jesus, who wants to occupy our souls
    completely.

130

And when we fail in this abandonment in God,
even in small things,
when we keep a place reserved for ourselves,
Jesus cannot take possession.
He cannot enter into us.
What is all this resistance we show?
What is all this rebellion,
this insistence on our own ideas,
this desire that we be the only ones
    who are right?
It is resistance to Jesus.
He cannot be Lord of every fiber of the heart
because some contain self-love,
which blocks His entrance.

This abandonment in the first place gives us
    great peace.
What are agitations, if not that we wanted one
    thing
and instead were contradicted?
We wanted things like this, a position like that,
and instead we were disregarded,
or things went in a way different from what
    we desired.
And so comes agitation,
and the person makes himself unhappy, torments
    himself.
The person who abandons himself in God
procures for himself a great peace.

If the Lord loves us —
and He does love us —
He will permit that in our lives
we will have to pass through difficult moments
and times, and perhaps through trials.
And even if temptations last for a long time,
and it turns out as it did for St. Teresa,
who remained burdened for fifteen years
with temptations and aridity;
if your spiritual state has to be such,
then your sanctity will be reached
only in this way: abandonment in God.

There can remain deep within us a repugnance
    to suffering,
to one thing or another,
but this does not impede our abandonment.
To feel something is not to consent to it.
If our will is really one with God's
— even when it seems that in the depths of our
    hearts
there is a battle raging against it;
if we perhaps feel our heart full of temptations,
of bad thoughts —
still we know that our will is with God.

Abandonment in God, therefore,
does not mean that one must exclude
and never have any more repugnance,
any more difficulties.

134

At times we must do as Jesus did in Gethsemane:
sweat blood in order to do the will of God
    totally.
But in the end, grace will triumph
and we will know how to embrace that which
    God wills.

It can happen, instead, that the Lord
will give you much serenity,
make your prayer sweet and easy,
and permit you to live in a place
where all love and respect you:
in this, too, abandonment in God, always....

Therefore, have great peace of soul.
Even if you feel as if you are in the deepest
    darkness,
nevertheless, feel a great peace.
Dying thus, in abandonment in God,
I think that one will have no purgatory,
or very little.
In this soul there is no more "self,"
but it is God who lives in him.

Faith is not complete if one lacks
the disposition to do the will of God,
whatever it may be.
But when faith is true
and there is love of God in one's heart,
God listens to his prayer
and gives him what is useful for his
    sanctification.

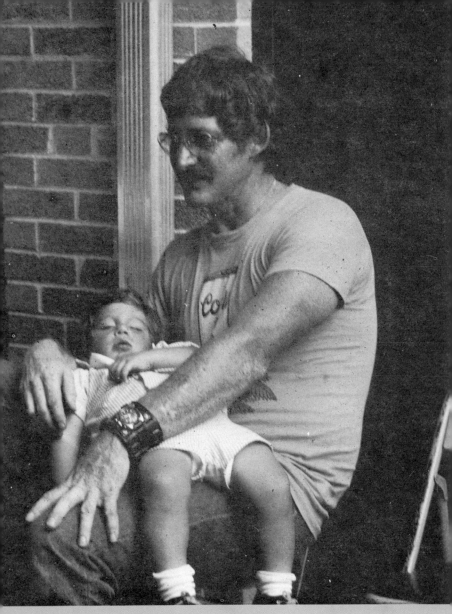

A beautiful poem says:
"As a little child rests secure
in the arms of his father,
thus the soul who has sincere faith
rests secure in the heart of God."

138

Remain in the hands of God
and when He has shown us His will,
by all means act decisively.
All our activity must be entrusted into
    God's hands....

Our attitude should be:
"Lord, I am your servant;
help me to know what You want."
Do we not sometimes usurp God's place?
Often, we say:
"I think..., I am..., I do...,"
but it is God who acts, not we.
Let's be like a pen which is there to be used.
We can take it when we wish,
write a word or many words with it,
but it will never protest to say:
"Why do you make me work so much?"
And when we put it aside,
it never demands the slightest thanks.

Do we have this abandonment in God?
If we want to make progress,
we will have to make a pretty long examination
    of conscience
on these points:
Do we still think differently than Jesus?
Do we still have sentiments differing from His?
Do we still have preferences and desires other
    than those of Jesus?
Do we dispose ourselves to conform to all
    Jesus desires?
In no other way will we reach perfection.

Really *live* by faith.
When there is truth and faith,
how much more profound will be the vision
    of God in paradise!
Here on earth there is faith;
but there, the vision.
And then, what joy in heaven!

What Faith

Can Do

Faith makes us look at life from the right
    perspective.
It makes us believe in paradise
and shows us the means to attain it:
prayer, a good life,
correspondence to our personal vocation,
and the fulfillment of our mission in life.

Faith makes us order our thoughts toward
      eternity;
it has us find continual means
of storing up treasures for everlasting life.
We are to place ourselves before the eternal truths,
before the two eternities which face us.
To live by faith means to keep present these
      great truths
and to order our entire lives according to
      these ends.
It means to read and study the catechesis
which the Church offers us
and to have faith in it.

Faith!
Faith which accompanies us in this invocation
　　we say:
"Virgin Mary, Mother of Jesus, make us saints!"
Yes, if you have faith,
you will become a saint!
The humble will be exalted.
But let us not look forward to exaltation
　　on this earth,
since that would be vanity.
Let us look forward,
instead, to our exaltation in heaven
where Jesus Christ has a place prepared for us.
Let us remain little, as we truly are in the
　　eyes of God,
so much in need of help and mercy.
And let us always be thankful to those
who are instruments in the hands of God
to enlighten us,
and are the salt which preserves us
from the corruption of sin.

Faith!
It makes us understand how poor
are the words of the men of this world,
and how precious, instead, is the wisdom
    of the Gospel.

Faith!
It fills our days with joy,
even though in their course we meet difficulties,
temptations, disillusionments.

Ask for the spirit of faith:
but ask for it continually
since it is the foundation, the root.

For the one who wants to approach God,
it is necessary to believe (cf. Heb. 5:5).
We can say here in the spiritual sense
that which Jesus Christ said to the woman
    (cf. Mk. 5:34):
"It is faith that saves."

Through faith we see all people as children
    of God
and our brothers in the "Our Father."

Through faith we see all people as souls
to whom we are debtors for truth,
good example, and prayer.

Through faith we see how Jesus Christ loved
    everyone,
especially the needy,
the sinners and the suffering.
He made no distinctions of a purely human kind,
but only on human-divine grounds.

Through faith we will have the right kind of
    nationalism.
In a nation we will always see souls especially
and their salvation—
never a nationalism contrary to the teachings
    of the Gospel,
and of a political or economic nature.
One desires that all be in conformity
with the pontifical doctrines:
laws, teachings,
morals, practice of religion.

"God shows no partiality," St. Peter said.
"Rather, the man of any nation
who fears God and acts uprightly
is acceptable to him."

—Acts 10:34-35

151

Through faith we see others
as fellow travelers toward eternity
and deduce from this view our duties of
mutual aid.

Through faith we understand the heart of the
    Divine Master,
who preaches and invites everyone to Himself:
"Come to me all of you."
We understand St. Paul,
"doctor of the gentiles,"
who in his great heart bore all men.
We understand Mary, Queen of Apostles,
who guides all the children of the heavenly
    Father
to Jesus, her divine Son and our Savior.

"Faith rests not on the wisdom of me

but on the power of God." —1 Corinthians 2:5

A Prayer of Faith

(attributed to Pope Clement XI)

Lord, I believe in You: increase my faith.
I trust in You: strengthen my trust.
I love You: let me love You more and more.
I am sorry for my sins: deepen my sorrow.

I worship You as my first beginning,
I long for You as my last end,
I praise You as my constant helper,
and call on You as my loving protector.

Guide me by Your wisdom, correct me with Your justice,
comfort me with Your mercy, protect me with your power.

I offer You, Lord, my thoughts: to be fixed on You;
my words: to have You for their theme;
my actions: to reflect my love for You;
my sufferings: to be endured for Your greater glory.

I want to do what You ask of me: in the way you ask,
for as long as You ask, because You ask it.

Lord, enlighten my understanding,
strengthen my will, purify my heart, and make me holy.

Help me to repent of my past sins
and to resist temptation in the future.
Help me to rise above my human weaknesses
and to grow stronger as a Christian.

Let me love You, my Lord and my God,
and see myself as I really am: a pilgrim in this world,
a Christian called to respect and love all whose lives I touch,
those in authority over me
or those under my authority,
my friends and my enemies.

Help me to conquer anger with gentleness,
greed by generosity, apathy by fervor.
Help me to forget myself and reach out toward others.

Make me prudent in planning, courageous in taking risks.
Make me patient in suffering, unassuming in prosperity.

Keep me, Lord, attentive at prayer,
temperate in food and drink,
diligent in my work, firm in my good intentions.

Let my conscience be clear, my conduct without fault,
my speech blameless, my life well-ordered.

Put me on guard against my human weaknesses.
Let me cherish Your love for me, keep Your law,
and come at last to Your salvation.

Teach me to realize that this world is passing,
that my true future is the happiness of heaven,
that life on earth is short, and the life to come eternal.

Help me to prepare for death with a proper fear of judgment,
but a greater trust in Your goodness.
Lead me safely through death to the endless joy of heaven.

Grant this through Christ our Lord. Amen.

Daughters of St. Paul

IN MASSACHUSETTS
    50 St. Paul's Avenue, Boston, Ma. 02130
    172 Tremont Street, Boston, Ma. 02111
IN NEW YORK
    78 Fort Place, Staten Island, N.Y. 10301
    59 East 43rd St., New York, N.Y. 10017
    625 East 187th Street, Bronx, N.Y. 10458
    525 Main Street, Buffalo, N.Y. 14203
IN NEW JERSEY
    Hudson Mall — Route 440 and
      Communipaw Ave., Jersey City, N.J. 07304
IN CONNECTICUT
    202 Fairfield Avenue, Bridgeport, Ct. 06604
IN OHIO
    2105 Ontario St. (at Prospect Ave.), Cleveland, Oh. 44115
    25 E. Eighth Street, Cincinnati, Oh. 45202
IN PENNSYLVANIA
    1719 Chestnut St., Philadelphia, Pa. 19103
IN FLORIDA
    2700 Biscayne Blvd., Miami, Fl. 33137
IN LOUISIANA
    4403 Veterans Memorial Blvd., Metairie, La. 70002
    1800 South Acadian Thruway, P.O. Box 2028,
      Baton Rouge, La. 70802
IN MISSOURI
    1001 Pine St. (at North 10th), St. Louis, Mo. 63101
IN TEXAS
    114 East Main Plaza, San Antonio, Tx. 78205
IN CALIFORNIA
    1570 Fifth Avenue, San Diego, Ca. 92101
    46 Geary Street, San Francisco, Ca. 94108
IN HAWAII
    1143 Bishop St., Honolulu, Hi. 96813
IN ALASKA
    750 West 5th Avenue, Anchorage, Ak. 99501
IN CANADA
    3022 Dufferin Street, Toronto 395, Ontario, Canada
IN ENGLAND
    57, Kensington Church Street, London W. 8, England
IN AUSTRALIA
    58, Abbotsford Rd., Homebush, N.S.W., Sydney 2140,
      Australia